The Complete
POCKET POSITIVES

An Anthology of Inspirational Thoughts

The Complete

POCKET POSITIVES

An Anthology of Inspirational Thoughts

Compiled by Maggie Pinkney

THE FIVE MILE PRESS

CONTENTS

Never Give Up

Face Up to Fear

Understand Sorrow, Understand Joy

Love is All You Need

Genius or Hard Work?

Begin by Believing

Always Be Yourself

Stop and Ponder Life's Meaning

Let Nature Enlarge Your Spirit

Lend a Helping Hand

You Can Do More Than You Think You Can...

INTRODUCTION

*There are two ways to live your life. One is as though nothing
is a miracle. The other is as though everything is a miracle.*

Albert Einstein, 1879–1955 GERMAN-BORN AMERICAN PHYSICIST

This life-affirming anthology taps into the thoughts of great scientists, statesmen, writers, philosophers, inventors and inspirational people from many other walks of life — providing a hotline to the combined wisdom of the centuries.

The wise and witty quotations included here cover a wide range of topics — from courage, goals, problems and persistence to friendship, relationships, happiness and success. But they all have one thing in common — they offer an optimistic view of human existence. Certain messages appear, clothed in different words and phrases, again and again. They urge us to develop enthusiasms, take action, face up to fears, never give up, believe in ourselves, not be daunted by mistakes of the past, and to regard each new day as a miracle.

Whenever you've had a bad day — and we all have them sometimes — dip into this collection of 'pocket positives' for guidance, comfort and encouragement. After you have read the words of such people as Calvin Coolidge, Mother Teresa, Henry Ford, Aung San Suu Kyi and Martin Luther King, things will soon fall into their proper perspective.

Some of these quotations are poetic and reflective. Others are pithy and to the point, but all are inspiring. This delightful collection demands to be browsed through again and again. On each reading you will find a different quotation that 'speaks' to you. If you take the sentiments expressed in this book to heart you will certainly enrich your life, and the lives of those around you.

Heed the words of the wise, and get more out of life!

THE POWER OF ENTHUSIASM

You can do anything if you have enthusiasm.
Enthusiasm is the yeast that makes your hopes rise to the stars.
Enthusiasm is the spark in your eye, the swing in your gait,
the grip of your hand, the irresistible surge of your will
and energy to execute your ideas...
Enthusiasm is at the bottom of all progress!

Henry Ford, 1863–1947   AMERICAN CAR MANUFACTURER

If you are not getting
as much from life as you want to,
then examine the state
of your enthusiasm.

Norman Vincent Peale, 1898–1993   AMERICAN WRITER AND MINISTER

I could not, at any age, be content to take my place

in a corner by the fireside and simply look on.

Life was meant to be lived. Curiosity must be kept alive.

The fatal thing is rejection. One must never, for whatever reason,

turn his back on life.

Eleanor Roosevelt, 1884–1962   First Lady of the United States of America, writer and diplomat

As life is action and passion,

it is required of man that he should share

the action and passion of his time,

at peril of being judged

not to have lived.

Oliver Wendell Holmes, 1809–1894 AMERICAN WRITER AND PHYSICIAN

Live all you can: it's a mistake not to.

It doesn't matter what you do in particular,

so long as you have had your life.

If you haven't had that,

what have you had?

Henry James, 1843–1916   AMERICAN NOVELIST

*T*he love of life is necessary

to the vigorous prosecution

of any undertaking.

Dr Samuel Johnson, 1709–1784   ENGLISH LEXICOGRAPHER, CRITIC AND ESSAYIST

Develop interest in life as you see it;

in people, things, literature, music —

the world is so rich, simply throbbing with rich treasures,

beautiful souls and interesting people.

Forget yourself.

Henry Miller, 1891–1980   AMERICAN AUTHOR

We act as though comfort and luxury were the chief requirements of life, when all we need to make us really happy is something to be enthusiastic about.

Charles Kingsley, 1819–1875   ENGLISH WRITER AND CLERGYMAN

You must learn day by day,

year by year, to broaden your horizons.

The more things you love, the more you are interested in,

the more you enjoy, the more you are indignant about,

the more you have left when anything happens.

Ethel Barrymore, 1879–1959   AMERICAN ACTRESS

HOLD ON TO YOUR DREAMS

Go confidently in the direction of your dreams! Live the life you've imagined.

Henry David Thoreau, 1817–1862   AMERICAN WRITER

It seems to me

we can never give up longing and wishing

for things while we are thoroughly alive.

There are certain things we feel

to be beautiful and good,

and we must hunger after them.

George Eliot (Mary Ann Evans), 1819–1880 ENGLISH NOVELIST

*T*hose who dream by day
are cognizant of many things
which escape those
who dream only
by night.

Edgar Allan Poe, 1809–1849 AMERICAN POET AND WRITER

The future belongs

to those who believe

in the beauty of

their dreams.

Eleanor Roosevelt, 1884–1962   FIRST LADY OF THE UNITED STATES OF AMERICA, WRITER AND DIPLOMAT

All big men are dreamers. They see things in the soft haze of a spring day or in the red fire of a long winter's evening. Some of us let great dreams die, but others nourish and protect them, nurse them through bad days till they bring them to the sunshine and light which comes always to those who sincerely hope that their dreams will come true.

Woodrow Wilson, 1856–1924   PRESIDENT OF THE UNITED STATES OF AMERICA

Always live your life with one dream to fulfil.

No matter how many of your dreams you have realised

in the past, always have a dream to go.

Because when you stop dreaming, life becomes

a mundane existence.

Sara Henderson, 1936-2005 AUSTRALIAN OUTBACK STATION MANAGER AND WRITER

*Some men see things as they are
and say 'Why?'
I dream things that never were
and say 'Why not?'*

George Bernard Shaw, 1856–1950   IRISH DRAMATIST, ESSAYIST AND CRITIC

CHERISH YOUR FRIENDS

We are all travellers

in the wilderness of this world,

and the best we can find in our travels

is an honest friend.

Robert Louis Stevenson, 1850–1894   SCOTTISH WRITER AND POET

I have learned that a good friend

is the purest of all God's gifts,

for it is a love that has

no exchange or payment.

Frances Farmer, 1910–1970   AMERICAN ACTRESS AND SINGER

*F*or whoever knows how

to return a kindness

he has received

must be a friend

above price.

Sophocles, c. 496–406 BC   GREEK TRAGEDIAN

A real friend

is one who walks in

when the rest of the world

walks out.

Walter Winchell, 1879–1972   AMERICAN JOURNALIST

I want someone to laugh with me,

someone to be grave with me,

someone to please me and help my discrimination

with his or her remark, and at times, no doubt,

to admire my acuteness and penetration.

Robert Burns, 1759–1796   SCOTTISH POET

One's friends are

that part of the human race

with which one can

be human.

George Santayana, 1863-1952   SPANISH PHILOSOPHER AND WRITER

Friendship consists

in forgetting

what one gives,

and remembering

what one receives.

Alexandre Dumas, 1803–1870   FRENCH NOVELIST

Under the magnetism of friendship

the modest man becomes bold;

the shy, confident;

the lazy, active;

or the impetuous, prudent and peaceful.

William Makepeace Thackeray, 1811–1863   ENGLISH WRITER

If a man does not make new acquaintance

as he advances through life,

he will soon find himself alone.

A man, sir, should keep his friendship

in constant repair.

Dr Samuel Johnson, 1709–1784   ENGLISH LEXICOGRAPHER, CRITIC AND ESSAYIST

Each new friend represents a world in us,

a world possibly not born until they arrive,

and it is only by this meeting

that a new world is born.

Anais Nin, 1903–1977   FRENCH NOVELIST

*W*e take care of our health, we lay up money,

we make our room tight, and our clothing sufficient;

but who provides wisely that he shall not be wanting

in the best property of all — friends?

Ralph Waldo Emerson, 1803–1882   AMERICAN ESSAYIST, POET AND PHILOSOPHER

And in the sweetness of friendship
let there be laughter,
and sharing of pleasures.
For in the dew of little things
the heart finds its morning
and is refreshed.

Kahlil Gibran, 1883–1931   LEBANESE POET, ARTIST AND MYSTIC

*F*riendship

improves happiness

and abates misery

by doubling our joy

and dividing our grief.

Joseph Addison, 1672–1719   ENGLISH ESSAYIST

SEEK MOMENTS
OF SOLITUDE

Solitude is as

needful to the imagination

as society is

wholesome for the character.

James Russell Lowell, 1819–1891   AMERICAN POET, ESSAYIST AND DIPLOMAT

Arranging a bowl of flowers in the morning
can give a sense of quiet in a crowded day —
like writing a poem or saying a prayer.
What matters is that one be for a time
inwardly attentive.

Anne Morrow Lindbergh, 1906-2001   AMERICAN WRITER

L*earn to get in touch*

with the silence within yourself

and know that everything in this life

has a purpose.

Elizabeth Kubler-Ross, 1926-2004 . SWISS-BORN AMERICAN PSYCHIATRIST AND WRITER

In solitude we give

passionate attention to our lives,

to our memories,

to the details around us.

Virginia Woolf, 1882–1941   ENGLISH NOVELIST

In meditation it is possible to dive deeper into the mind to a place where there is no disturbance and there is absolute solitude. It is at this point in the profound stillness that the sound of the mind can be heard.

A. E. I. Falconar, b. 1926   INDIAN-BORN PHILOSOPHER

O Solitude,

the soul's best friend,

That man acquainted with himself

dost make.

Charles Cotton, 1630–1687   ENGLISH POET

*Solitude is the nurse
of enthusiasm,
and enthusiasm is the true parent
of genius.*

Isaac D'Israeli, 1766–1848   ENGLISH LITERARY CRITIC

One of the pleasantest things
in the world is going on a journey;
but I like to go by myself.

William Hazlitt, 1778–1830 · BRITISH ESSAYIST

I am sure of this, that by going much alone

a man will get more of a noble courage

in thought and word

than from all the wisdom

that is in books.

Ralph Waldo Emerson, 1803–1882   AMERICAN ESSAYIST, POET AND PHILOSOPHER

Shoot for the Moon

Shoot for the moon.

Even if you miss it

you will land among

the stars.

Lester Louis Brown, b. 1928   AMERICAN JOURNALIST

Far away there in the sunshine

are my highest aspirations.

I may not reach them but I can look up

and see their beauty, believe in them

and try to follow them.

Louisa May Alcott, 1832–1888   AMERICAN NOVELIST

If you aspire to the highest place,
it is no disgrace to stop at the second
or even the third place.

Cicero, 106–43 BC   ROMAN ORATOR, STATESMAN AND ESSAYIST

*S*et your sights high, the higher the better.

Expect the most wonderful things to happen,

not in the future but right now.

Realise that nothing is too good.

Allow absolutely nothing to hamper you

or hold you up in any way.

Eileen Caddy, CO-FOUNDER OF THE FINDHORN FOUNDATION, SCOTLAND

Never look down to test the ground

before taking your next step;

only he who keeps his eye fixed on the far horizon

will find his right road.

Dag Hammarskjöld, 1905–1961   SWEDISH STATESMAN AND SECRETARY-GENERAL OF THE UNITED NATIONS

Our aspirations are our possibilities.

Dr Samuel Johnson, 1709–1784   ENGLISH LEXICOGRAPHER, CRITIC AND ESSAYIST

*W*hen goals go, meaning goes.

When meaning goes, purpose goes.

When purpose goes,

life goes dead on our hands.

Carl Jung, 1875–1961   SWISS PSYCHIATRIST

ATTITUDE CAN SHAPE YOUR LIFE

It is worth a thousand pounds a year to have the habit of looking on the bright side of things.

Dr Samuel Johnson, 1709–1784   ENGLISH LEXICOGRAPHER, CRITIC AND ESSAYIST

No pessimist ever discovered

the secrets of the stars,

or sailed to an uncharted land,

or opened a new heaven

to the horizon of the spirit.

Helen Keller, 1880–1968   DEAF AND BLIND AMERICAN WRITER AND SCHOLAR

*The mind is its own place,
and in itself
Can make a heaven of hell,
a hell of heaven.*

John Milton, 1606–1674   ENGLISH POET

The greater part of our happiness or misery

depends on our dispositions and not on our circumstances.

We carry the seeds of the one or the other

about with us in our minds wherever we go.

Martha Washington, 1731–1802   FIRST LADY OF THE UNITED STATES OF AMERICA

A positive thinker does not refuse to recognise
the negative, he refuses to dwell on it.
Positive thinking is a form of thought which habitually
looks for the best results from the worst conditions.

Norman Vincent Peale, 1898–1993   AMERICAN WRITER AND MINISTER

*Make the most of the best
and the least of the worst.*

Robert Louis Stevenson, 1850–1894   SCOTTISH WRITER AND POET

Over the winter glaciers

I see the summer glow;

And through the wild-piled snowdrift

The warm rosebuds below.

Ralph Waldo Emerson, 1803–1882   AMERICAN ESSAYIST, POET AND PHILOSOPHER

In the midst of winter,

I finally learned

there was in me

an invincible summer.

Albert Camus, 1913–1960   FRENCH WRITER

The greatest revolution of our generation

is the discovery that human beings,

by changing the inner attitudes of their minds,

can change the outer aspects of their lives.

William James, 1842–1910   AMERICAN PSYCHOLOGIST AND PHILOSOPHER

PROBLEMS ARE FOR SOLVING

*If there were nothing wrong in the world,
there wouldn't be anything for us to do.*

George Bernard Shaw, 1856–1950   IRISH DRAMATIST, ESSAYIST AND CRITIC

I'm grateful for all my problems.

As each of them was overcome

I became stronger and more able

to meet those yet to come.

I grew on my difficulties.

J. C. Penney, 1875–1971   AMERICAN RETAILING MAGNATE

A problem well stated is a problem half solved.

Charles Franklin Kettering, 1876–1958 AMERICAN ENGINEER AND INVENTOR

Problems are a major part of life.

Don't whinge about why you always have problems...

Get on with the solving.

Take it from someone who has been there —

the solving gets easier as you go along.

Sara Henderson, 1936-2005   AUSTRALIAN OUTBACK STATION MANAGER AND WRITER

I think these difficult times

have helped me to understand better than before

how infinitely rich and beautiful life is in every way

and that so many things one goes around worrying about

are of no importance whatsoever.

Isak Dinesen (Karen Blixen), 1885–1962   DANISH WRITER

Problems call forth our courage and our wisdom;
indeed, they create our courage and our wisdom.
It is only because of problems that we grow mentally
and spiritually. It is through the pain of
confronting and resolving problems
that we learn.

M. Scott Peck, b. 1936   AMERICAN PSYCHIATRIST AND WRITER

Those things that hurt, instruct.

Benjamin Franklin, 1706–1790   AMERICAN STATESMAN AND SCIENTIST

Life affords no higher pleasure than that of surmounting difficulties, passing from one step of success to another, forming new wishes and seeing them gratified.

Dr Samuel Johnson, 1709–1784   ENGLISH LEXICOGRAPHER, CRITIC AND ESSAYIST

I could do nothing without my problems;

they toughen my mind. In fact I tell my assistants

not to bring me their succcesses for they weaken me;

but rather to bring me their problems,

for they strengthen me.

Charles Franklin Kettering, 1876–1958   AMERICAN ENGINEER AND INVENTOR

MAKE THE MOST OF YOUR MISTAKES

Some of the best lessons we ever learn,
we learn from our mistakes and failures.
The error of the past is the success and
wisdom of the future.

Tyron Edwards, 1861–1941   AMERICAN THEOLOGIAN

I have learned more from my mistakes than from my successes.

Sir Humphry Davy, 1778–1829   ENGLISH CHEMIST AND INVENTOR

Even a mistake
may turn out to be the one thing
necessary to a worthwhile achievement.

Henry Ford, 1863–1947   AMERICAN CAR MANUFACTURER

If you have made mistakes...
there is always another chance for you.
You may have a fresh start at any moment
you choose, for this thing we call 'failure' is not
the falling down, but the staying down.

Mary Pickford, 1893–1979   AMERICAN ACTRESS

When we begin to take our failures non-seriously,

it means we are ceasing to be afraid of them.

It is of immense importance to learn

to laugh at ourselves.

Katherine Mansfield, 1888–1923   NEW ZEALAND SHORT STORY WRITER

We learn wisdom from failure much more than success.

We often discover what we WILL do,

by finding out what we will NOT do.

Samuel Smiles, 1812–1904   SCOTTISH AUTHOR AND SOCIAL REFORMER

Anyone who has never made a mistake

has never tried anything new.

Albert Einstein, 1879–1955   GERMAN-BORN AMERICAN PHYSICIST

You know, by the time you've reached my age, you've made plenty of mistakes if you've lived your life properly.

Ronald Reagan, 1911-2005   PRESIDENT OF THE UNITED STATES OF AMERICA

Nobody makes a greater mistake

than he who does nothing

because he could do so little.

Edmund Burke, 1729–1797   BRITISH POLITICIAN

JUST
DO IT!

I have spent my days stringing and

unstringing my instrument,

while the song I came to sing remains unsung.

Rabindranath Tagore, 1861–1941   INDIAN POET AND PHILOSOPHER

Do the thing

and you will have

the power.

Ralph Waldo Emerson, 1803–1882 AMERICAN ESSAYIST, POET AND PHILOSOPHER

Our great business in life

is not to see what lies dimly at a distance,

but to do what lies clearly at hand.

Thomas Carlyle, 1795–1881   Scottish essayist, historian and philosopher

You can't build a reputation

on what you're going to do.

Henry Ford, 1863–1947   AMERICAN CAR MANUFACTURER

Action is the antidote to despair.

Joan Baez, b. 1941   AMERICAN FOLK SINGER

Don't be afraid to take a big step
if one is indicated.
You can't cross a chasm
in two small jumps.

David Lloyd George, 1863–1945   BRITISH PRIME MINISTER AND STATESMAN

Sometimes the only way for me to find out what it is I want to do is go ahead and do something. Then the moment I start to act, my feelings become clear.

Hugh Prather, b. 1938   AMERICAN WRITER

The great end of life

is not knowledge,

but action.

Thomas Fuller, 1608–1661   ENGLISH CLERGYMAN AND WRITER

*A*ction may not always bring happiness,

but there is no happiness without action.

Benjamin Disraeli, 1804–1881   BRITISH PRIME MINISTER AND WRITER

Don't wait for a light to appear

at the end of the tunnel,

stride down there...

and light the bloody thing yourself.

Sara Henderson, 1936-2005 AUSTRALIAN OUTBACK STATION MANAGER AND WRITER

A little knowledge that acts

is worth infinitely more

than knowledge that is idle.

Kahlil Gibran, 1883–1931   LEBANESE POET, ARTIST AND MYSTIC

NEVER
GIVE UP

When I was a young man, I observed that nine out of ten things I did were failures. I didn't want to be a failure, so I did ten times more work.

George Bernard Shaw, 1856–1950   IRISH DRAMATIST, WRITER AND CRITIC

Character consists of what you do on the third and fourth tries.

James A. Michener, 1907–1997   AMERICAN WRITER

We haven't failed.

We now know a thousand things that won't work,

so we're that much closer to finding what will.

Thomas Edison, 1847–1931   AMERICAN INVENTOR

Nothing in this world can take the place of persistence. Talent will not; nothing is more common than unsuccessful men with talent.

Genius will not; unrewarded genius is almost a proverb.

Education will not; the world is full of educated failures.

Persistence and determination alone are omnipotent.

Calvin Coolidge, 1872–1933 PRESIDENT OF THE UNITED STATES OF AMERICA

*T*o keep a lamp burning

we have to keep putting oil in it.

Mother Teresa of Calcutta, 1910–1997   Yugoslav-born missionary

When you get into a tight place and everything goes against you,

till it seems as though you could not hang on a minute longer,

never give up then, for that is just the place and time

that the tide will turn.

Harriet Beecher Stowe, 1811–1896   AMERICAN AUTHOR AND SOCIAL REFORMER

Consider the postage stamp;

its usefulness consists in the ability

to stick to one thing till it gets there.

Josh Billings, 1818–1885   AMERICAN WRITER

FACE UP
TO FEAR

Fear is a question.
What are you afraid of and why?
Our fears are a treasure house of
self-knowledge if we explore them.

Marilyn French, b. 1929   AMERICAN NOVELIST

I have a lot of things to prove to myself.

One is that I can live my life fearlessly.

Oprah Winfrey, b. 1954   AMERICAN TELEVISION PERSONALITY

Do the thing you fear and the death of fear is certain.

Ralph Waldo Emerson, 1803–1882   AMERICAN ESSAYIST, POET AND PHILOSOPHER

Courage faces fear and thereby masters it. Cowardice represses fear and is thereby mastered by it.

Martin Luther King, Jr, 1929–1968   AMERICAN CIVIL RIGHTS LEADER AND MINISTER

Life is either a daring adventure or nothing.
To keep our faces toward change and behave
like free spirits in the presence of fate
is strength undefeatable.

Helen Keller, 1880–1968   BLIND AND DEAF AMERICAN WRITER AND SCHOLAR

*Life shrinks or expands
in proportion to one's courage.*

Anais Nin, 1903–1977 FRENCH NOVELIST

Facing it, always facing it.

That's the way to get through.

Face it.

Joseph Conrad, 1856–1924 POLISH-BORN BRITISH WRITER

Of all the liars in the world,

sometimes the worst are your own fears.

Rudyard Kipling, 1865–1936   ENGLISH POET AND AUTHOR

*W*ithin a system which denies the existence of basic human rights, fear tends to be the order of the day. Yet even under the most crushing state machinery, courage rises up again and again, for fear is not the natural state of civilised man.

Aung San Suu Kyi, b. 1945   BURMA'S DEMOCRATICALLY ELECTED LEADER

I believe anyone can conquer fear

by doing the things he fears to do,

provided he keeps on doing them

until he gets a record of

successful experiences behind him.

Eleanor Roosevelt, 1884–1962   FIRST LADY OF THE UNITED STATES OF AMERICA, WRITER AND DIPLOMAT

When I became ill, the years of pain and confusion loomed up like some primitive monster of the deep...I lived in fear of dying. The strange paradox is that by confronting my fear of death, I found myself and created a new life.

Lucia Capacchione   AMERICAN ART THERAPIST

Courage is resistance to fear,

mastery of fear,

not absence of fear.

Mark Twain, 1835–1910   AMERICAN WRITER AND HUMORIST

The bravest thing you can do
when you are not brave
is to profess courage
and act accordingly.

Corra May White Harris, 1869–1935   AMERICAN WRITER

UNDERSTAND SORROW, UNDERSTAND JOY

The deeper the sorrow that carves into your being,

the more joy you can contain. Joy and sorrow are inseparable.

Kahlil Gibran, 1883–1931   LEBANESE POET, ARTIST AND MYSTIC

Truly, it is in the darkness that one finds

the light, so when we are in sorrow,

then this light is nearest to us.

Johannes Eckhart, c. 1260–1327   GERMAN MYSTIC

Where there is sorrow

there is holy ground.

Oscar Wilde, 1854–1900   Irish dramatist, novelist and wit

Have courage for the greatest sorrows

of life and patience for the small ones,

and when you have laboriously accomplished

your daily tasks, go to sleep in peace.

God is awake.

Victor Hugo, 1802–1885   FRENCH POET AND WRITER

Strength is born in the deep silence of long-suffering hearts; not amid joy.

When it is dark enough,

you can see the stars.

Ralph Waldo Emerson, 1803–1882   AMERICAN ESSAYIST, POET AND PHILOSOPHER

*P*ure and complete sorrow

is as impossible

as pure and complete joy.

Leo Tolstoy, 1828–1910   RUSSIAN NOVELIST

Blessed are they that mourn,

for they shall be comforted.

Matthew 5:4

Never to suffer would be

never to have been blessed.

Edgar Allan Poe, 1809–1849   AMERICAN POET AND WRITER

'On with the dance!

Let joy be unconfined' is my motto,

whether there's any dance to dance

or joy to unconfine.

Mark Twain, 1835–1910   AMERICAN WRITER AND HUMORIST

Who will tell whether one happy moment of love,

or the joy of breathing or walking on a bright

morning and smelling the fresh air, is not worth

all the suffering and effort which life implies?

Erich Fromm, 1900–1980   AMERICAN PSYCHOANALYST

LOVE IS ALL YOU NEED

To love means never to be afraid of the windstorms of life; should you shield the canyons from the windstorms you would never see the beauty of the carvings.

Elizabeth Kubler-Ross, 1926-2004   SWISS-BORN AMERICAN PSYCHIATRIST AND WRITER

Treasure the love that you receive above all.
It will survive long after your gold and
good health have vanished.

Og *Mandino,* 1923-1996 AMERICAN AUTHOR

*T*he only thing I know about love

is that love is all there is...

Love can do all but raise the dead.

Emily Dickinson, 1830–1886   AMERICAN POET

Love is a fruit in season at all times,
and within the reach of every hand.
Anyone may gather it and no limit is set.
Everyone can reach this love through meditation,
spirit of prayer, and sacrifice,
by an intense inner life.

Mother Teresa of Calcutta, 1910–1997   YUGOSLAV-BORN MISSIONARY

One word frees us of all the weight and pain of life; that word is love.

Sophocles, 496–406 BC GREEK TRAGEDIAN

*I*n our life there is a single colour,

as on an artist's palette, which provides

the meaning of life and art.

It is the colour of love.

Marc Chagall, 1887–1985   FRENCH ARTIST

Love is patient, love is kind.

It does not envy, it does not boast, it is not proud.

It is not rude, it is not self-seeking, it is not easily angered,

it keeps no records of wrongs.

Corinthians 13: 4-5

There is a land of the living
and a land of the dead,
and the bridge is love.

Thornton Wilder, 1897–1975   AMERICAN AUTHOR AND DRAMATIST

If we make our goal to live a life of compassion and unconditional love, then the world will indeed become a garden where all kinds of flowers can bloom and grow.

Elisabeth Kübler-Ross, b. 1926   SWISS-BORN AMERICAN PSYCHIATRIST AND WRITER

Genius or Hard Work?

A genius! For thirty-seven years

I've practised fourteen hours a day,

and now they call me a genius!

Pablo Sarasate, 1844–1908   SPANISH VIOLINIST AND COMPOSER

The secret of genius is to carry the spirit

of the child into old age, which means

never losing your enthusiasm.

Aldous Huxley, 1894–1963   ENGLISH WRITER

Every production of genius

must be the production

of enthusiasm.

Benjamin Disraeli, 1804–1881   ENGLISH PRIME MINISTER AND WRITER

Genius is nothing but labour and diligence.

William Hogarth, 1697–1764   ENGLISH PAINTER AND POLITICAL CARICATURIST

To believe your own thought,

to believe that what is true for you

in your private heart is true for all men

— that is genius.

Ralph Waldo Emerson, 1803–1882   AMERICAN ESSAYIST, POET AND PHILOSOPHER

Genius is one percent inspiration and ninety-nine percent perspiration.

Thomas A. Edison, 1847–1931   AMERICAN INVENTOR

Men give me credit for some genius. All the genius I have is this: when I have a subject in mind, I study it profoundly. Day and night it is before me. My mind becomes pervaded with it...the effort which I have made is what people are pleased to call genius. It is the fruit of labour and thought.

Alexander Hamilton, 1755–1804   AMERICAN STATESMAN

One is not born a genius,

one becomes a genius.

Simone de Beauvoir, 1908–1986   FRENCH WRITER

If people knew how hard I work to gain my mastery,

it would not seem so wonderful at all.

Michelangelo, 1475–1564   ITALIAN PAINTER AND SCULPTOR

BEGIN BY BELIEVING

They are able who think they are able.

Virgil, 70–19 BC   ROMAN POET

The thing always happens

that you really believe in;

and the belief in a thing

makes it happen.

Frank Lloyd Wright, 1869–1959   AMERICAN ARCHITECT

The secret of making something work in your lives is first of all, the deep desire to make it work; then the faith and belief that it can work; then to hold that clear definite vision in your consciousness and see it working out step by step, without one thought of doubt or disbelief.

Eileen Caddy CO-FOUNDER OF THE FINDHORN FOUNDATION, SCOTLAND

One of the greatest of all principles

is that men can do

what they think they can do.

Norman Vincent Peale, 1898–1993   AMERICAN WRITER AND MINISTER

I knew I was going to be a comedian when I was about six. You get what you believe you'll get. You have to really want it and you'll get it.

Billy Connolly, b. 1942   SCOTTISH COMEDIAN

Believe that life is worth living,

and your belief will help create the fact.

William James, 1842–1910   American psychologist and philosopher

To accomplish great things we must

not only act, but also dream;

not only plan, but also believe.

Whether you believe you can do a thing

or believe you can't,

you are right.

Henry Ford, 1863–1947   AMERICAN CAR MANUFACTURER

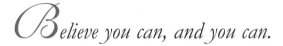

Believe you can, and you can.

Belief is one of the most powerful of all problem dissolvers.

When you believe that a difficulty can be overcome,

you are more than halfway to victory over it already.

Norman Vincent Peale, 1898–1993   AMERICAN WRITER AND MINISTER

ALWAYS BE
YOURSELF

I was born a jackdaw;

why should I be an owl?

Ogden Nash, 1902–1971   AMERICAN HUMOROUS POET

Always be a first-rate version of yourself,

instead of a second-rate version of somebody else.

Judy Garland, 1922–1969   AMERICAN SINGER

If I try to be like him,

who will be like me?

Jewish proverb

Every individual has a place to fill in the world,

and is important, in some respect,

whether he chooses to be or not.

Nathaniel Hawthorne, 1804–1864   AMERICAN NOVELIST

What is right for one soul may not be right for another. It may mean having to stand on your own and do something strange in the eyes of others. But do not be daunted. Do whatever it is because you know within it is right for you.

Eileen Caddy   CO-FOUNDER OF THE FINDHORN FOUNDATION, SCOTLAND

To be nobody but yourself — in a world which

is doing its best, night and day, to make you like

everybody else — means to fight the hardest battle

which any human being can fight,

and never stop fighting.

---

e.e. cummings, 1894–1962 ENGLISH POET

This above all — to thine own self be true,

And it must follow, as night follows day,

Thou canst not then be false to any man.

William Shakespeare, 1564–1616   ENGLISH PLAYWRIGHT AND POET

Don't surrender your individuality, which is your greatest

agent of power, to the customs and conventionalities

that have got their life from the great mass...

Do you want to be a power in the world?

Then be yourself.

Ralph Waldo Trine, 1866–1958   AMERICAN POET AND WRITER

What's man's first duty?

The answer's brief: to be himself.

Henrik Ibsen, 1828–1906 NORWEGIAN WRITER, DRAMATIST AND POET

It isn't until you come to a spiritual understanding of who you are — not necessarily a religious feeling, but deep down, the spirit within — that you can begin to take control.

Oprah Winfrey, b. 1954   AMERICAN TELEVISION PERSONALITY

Resolve to be thyself; and know that he

Who finds himself, loses his misery.

Matthew Arnold, 1822–1888   BRITISH WRITER

Being myself includes taking risks with myself, taking risks on new behaviour, trying new ways of 'being myself', so that I can see who it is I want to be.

Hugh Prather, b. 1938   AMERICAN WRITER

One has just to be oneself. That's my basic message. The moment you accept yourself as you are, all burdens, all mountainous burdens, simply disappear. Then life is a sheer joy, a festival of lights.

Bhagwan Shree Rajneesh, 1931-1990 INDIAN SPIRITUAL MASTER

STOP AND PONDER
LIFE'S MEANING

At the end of your life, you will never regret

not having passed one more test, not winning

one more verdict or not closing one more deal.

You will regret time not spent with a husband,

a friend, a child or parent.

Barbara Bush, b. 1925   FIRST LADY OF THE UNITED STATES OF AMERICA

The purpose of life is to matter — to count, to stand for something, to have it make some difference that we lived at all.

Leo Rosten, 1908-1997   POLISH-BORN AMERICAN WRITER AND HUMORIST

The greatest use of life is to spend it
for something that will outlast it.

William James, 1842–1910   AMERICAN PSYCHOLOGIST AND PHILOSOPHER

*N*o man can live happily who regards himself alone,

who turns everything to his own advantage.

Thou must live for another if thou wishest

to live for thyself.

Seneca, c. 4 BC–65 AD   ROMAN PHILOSOPHER, DRAMATIST AND STATESMAN

*He who does not live in some degree for others,
hardly lives for himself.*

Michel de Montaigne, 1533–1592 FRENCH ESSAYIST

You must understand the whole of life, not just

one little part of it. That is why you must read,

that is why you must look at the skies, that is why

you must sing and dance, and write poems, and suffer;

and understand, for all that is life.

Jiddu Krishnamurti, 1895–1986   INDIAN THEOSOPHIST

There are two things to aim for in life:

first to get what you want; and, after that, to enjoy it.

Only the wisest of mankind achieve the second.

Logan Pearsall Smith, 1865–1946   AMERICAN-BORN BRITISH WIT, WRITER AND CRITIC

Each player must accept the cards life deals him.
But once they are in hand, he alone must decide
how to play the cards in order to win the game.

Voltaire, 1694–1778   FRENCH PHILOSOPHER AND AUTHOR

Life is not made up of great sacrifices and duties but of little things in which smiles and kindness given habitually are what win and preserve the heart and secure comfort.

Sir Humphry Davy, 1778–1829   ENGLISH CHEMIST AND INVENTOR

We have to steer our true life's course. Whatever your calling is in life! The whole purpose of being here is to figure out what that is as soon as possible, so you go about the business of being on track, of not being owned by what your mother said, what society said, whatever people think a woman is supposed to be...when you can exceed other people's expectations and be defined by your own!

Oprah Winfrey, b. 1954   AMERICAN TELEVISION PERSONALITY

I have never given very deep thought to a philosophy of life, though I have a few ideas that I think are useful to me:

Do whatever comes your way as well as you can.

Think as little as possible about yourself.

Think as much as possible about other people.

Dwell on things that are interesting.

Since you get more joy out of giving joy to others you should put a good deal of thought into the happiness that you are able to give.

Eleanor Roosevelt, 1884–1962   First Lady of the United States of America, writer and diplomat

*I*s it so small a thing

To have enjoy'd the sun,

To have liv'd light

In the spring,

To have lov'd, to have thought, to have done?

Matthew Arnold, 1822–1888   ENGLISH POET AND ESSAYIST

As long as you live,
keep learning how to live.

Seneca, c. 4 BC–65 AD   ROMAN DRAMATIST, POET AND STATESMAN

LET NATURE
ENLARGE YOUR SPIRIT

Come forth into the light of things,
Let Nature be your teacher.

William Wordsworth, 1770–1850   BRITISH POET

There can be no very black misery
to him who lives in the midst of nature
and has his senses still.

Henry David Thoreau, 1817–1862   AMERICAN WRITER

*A*ll through my life,

the new sights of Nature

made me rejoice like a child.

Marie Curie, 1867–1934   POLISH-BORN FRENCH CHEMIST

*After you have exhausted what there is
in business, politics, conviviality and so on —
what remains? Nature remains.*

Walt Whitman, 1819–1892   AMERICAN POET

Nature never did betray the heart that loved her.

William Wordsworth, 1770–1850   BRITISH POET

There is a pleasure in the pathless woods,

There is a rapture on the lonely shore,

There is society, where none intrudes,

By the deep Sea, and music in its roar.

I love not Man the less, but Nature more.

Lord Byron, 1788–1824   ENGLISH POET

Love all God's creation, both the whole and every grain of sand. Love every leaf, every ray of light. Love the animals, love the plants, love each separate thing. If thou love each thing thou wilt perceive the mystery of God in all...

Feodor Dostoevsky, 1821–1881   RUSSIAN NOVELIST

*E*very part of this earth is sacred to my people.

Every shining pine needle, every sandy shore,

Every mist in the dark woods, every clearing

and every humming insect is holy in

the memory of my people.

Chief Seathl   FROM A LETTER WRITTEN IN 1883 TO THE PRESIDENT OF THE UNITED STATES OF AMERICA

Those undescribed, ambrosial mornings when a thousand birds were heard gently twittering and ushering in the light, like the argument to a new canto of an epic and heroic poem. The serenity, the infinite promise of such a morning...

Henry David Thoreau, 1817–1862   AMERICAN WRITER

LEND A
HELPING HAND

Hands that help are holier than lips that pray.

Sai Baba INDIAN SPIRITUAL MASTER

*D*o something for somebody every day

for which you do not get paid.

Albert Schweitzer, 1875–1965   FRENCH MEDICAL MISSIONARY

Doing nothing for others is the undoing of one's self. We must be purposely kind and generous or we miss the best part of life's existence. The heart that goes out of itself gets large and full of joy. We do ourselves most good by doing something for others.

Horace Mann, 1796–1859   AMERICAN EDUCATOR, WRITER AND POLITICIAN

It is one of the most beautiful compensations

of this life that no man can sincerely try

to help another without helping himself.

Ralph Waldo Emerson, 1803–1882   AMERICAN ESSAYIST, POET AND PHILOSOPHER

The best way to cheer yourself up is to cheer someone else up.

Mark Twain, 1835–1910   AMERICAN WRITER AND HUMORIST

*W*e can be cured of depression in only
fourteen days if every day we will try to think
of how we can be helpful to others.

Alfred Adler, 1870–1937   AUSTRIAN PSYCHIATRIST

I expect to pass through life but once.

If, therefore, there be any kindness I can show,

or any good thing I can do to any fellow being,

let me do it now, for I shall not pass this way again.

William Penn, 1644–1718   ENGLISH QUAKER AND FOUNDER OF PENNSYLVANIA, USA

Little deeds of kindness,

Little words of love,

Help to make earth happy

Like the heaven above.

Julia Fletcher Carney, 1823–1908   AMERICAN TEACHER

If someone listens, or stretches out a hand

or whispers a word of encouragement,

or attempts to understand a lonely person,

extraordinary things begin to happen.

Loretta Firzaris, b. 1920   AMERICAN EDUCATOR AND WRITER

You Can Do More Than You Think You Can ...

Love not what you are but what you may become.

Miguel de Cervantes, 1547–1616   SPANISH WRITER

If we did all the things

we are capable of doing we would

truly astound ourselves.

Thomas Edison, 1847–1931   AMERICAN INVENTOR

We should say to each [child]:
Do you know what you are? You are a marvel.
You are unique...You may become a Shakespeare,
a Michelangelo, a Beethoven.
You have the capacity for anything.

Pablo Casals, 1876–1973   SPANISH CELLIST, CONDUCTOR AND COMPOSER

*I have tried to write the best I can;
sometimes I have good luck and
write better than I can.*

Ernest Hemingway, 1898–1961   AMERICAN WRITER

No matter what your level of ability,
you have more potential than you can
ever develop in a lifetime.

Anonymous

Compared to what we ought to be we are only half awake. We are making use of only a small part of our physical and mental resources. Stating the thing broadly, the human individual thus lives far within his limits. He possesses power of various sorts which he habitually fails to use.

William James, 1842–1910   AMERICAN PSYCHOLOGIST AND PHILOSOPHER

I tell you that as long as I can conceive something better than myself I cannot be easy unless I am striving to bring it into existence or clearing the way for it.

George Bernard Shaw, 1856–1950   IRISH DRAMATIST, WRITER AND CRITIC

To be what we are,

and to become what we are capable of becoming is

the only end in life.

Robert Louis Stevenson, 1850–1894   SCOTTISH AUTHOR AND POET

There's only one corner of the universe you can be certain of improving, and that's your own self.

Aldous Huxley, 1894–1963   ENGLISH WRITER

LEARN TO FORGIVE

A quarrel between friends, when made up,

adds a new tie to friendship, as experience shows

that the callosity formed around a broken bone

makes it stronger than before.

St Francis de Sales, 1567–1622   FRENCH THEOLOGIAN

*T*he forgiving state of mind is a
magnetic power for attracting good.
No good thing can be withheld from
the forgiving state of mind.

Catherine Ponder   AMERICAN MOTIVATIONAL SPEAKER

The man who opts for revenge
should dig two graves.

Chinese proverb

He that cannot forgive others breaks

the bridge over which he must pass himself;

for every man has need to be forgiven.

Thomas Fuller, 1608–1661   ENGLISH CLERGYMAN AND WRITER

The reason to forgive is for your own sake.

For our own health. Because beyond that point needed

for healing, if we hold on to our anger we stop growing

and our souls begin to shrivel.

M. Scott Peck, b. 1936   AMERICAN PSYCHIATRIST AND WRITER

*F*or my part, I believe in the forgiveness
of sins and the redemption of ignorance.

Adlai Stevenson, 1900–1965   AMERICAN LAWYER, STATESMAN AND UNITED NATIONS REPRESENTATIVE

*Forgive us our trespasses
as we forgive them
that trespass against us.*

The Lord's Prayer

One forgives as much

as one loves.

Duc de la Rochefoucauld, 1616–1680   FRENCH WRITER

Forgiveness is not an occasional act,
it is a permanent attitude.

Martin Luther King, Jr, 1929–1968   AMERICAN CIVIL RIGHTS LEADER AND MINISTER

MAKE YOUR OWN HAPPINESS

Most people are about as happy as they make up their minds to be.

Abraham Lincoln, 1809–1865   PRESIDENT OF THE UNITED STATES OF AMERICA

*O*ne is happy as a result of one's own efforts, once one knows

the necessary ingredients of happiness — simple tastes,

a certain degree of courage, self-denial to a point,

love of work, and above all, a clear conscience.

Happiness is no vague dream.

George Sand (Amandine Aurore Lucie Dupin), 1804–1876   FRENCH NOVELIST

The great essentials to happiness in this life are something to do, something to love and something to hope for.

Joseph Addison, 1672–1719   ENGLISH ESSAYIST

Happiness is a butterfly which, when pursued,

is always beyond our grasp, but which,

if you sit down quietly, may alight upon you.

Nathaniel Hawthorne, 1804–1864   AMERICAN WRITER

The happiest people seem to be those who are producing something; the bored people are those who are consuming much and producing nothing.

William Inge, 1860–1954   ENGLISH PRELATE AND WRITER

The secret of happiness is not in doing what one likes, but in liking what one has to do.

J. M. Barrie, 1860–1937   SCOTTISH WRITER AND DRAMATIST

If you want to understand the meaning of happiness,

you must see it as a reward and not as a goal.

Antoine de Saint-Exupery, 1900–1944   FRENCH WRITER AND AVIATOR

If only we'd stop trying to be happy,
we could have a pretty good time.

Edith Wharton, 1862–1937   American novelist

Happiness arises in the first place from the enjoyment of one's self, and, in the next, from the friendship and conversations with a few select companions.

Joseph Addison, 1672–1719   ENGLISH ESSAYIST

The happiness of life is made up of minute fractions. The little soon forgotten charities of a kiss or smile, a kind look, a heartfelt compliment — countless infinitesimals of pleasurable and genial feelings.

Samuel Taylor Coleridge, 1772–1834 ENGLISH POET

I don't know what your destiny will be; but one thing I know: the only ones among you who will be really happy are those who will have sought and found how to serve.

Albert Schweitzer, 1875–1965   FRENCH MEDICAL MISSIONARY

SECRETS OF SUCCESS

Singleness of purpose is one of

the chief essentials for success in life,

no matter what may be one's aims.

John D. Rockefeller, Jr, 1874–1960   AMERICAN OIL MILLIONAIRE AND PHILANTHROPIST

All successful people have a goal.
No one can get anywhere unless
he knows where he wants to go
and what he wants to do.

Norman Vincent Peale, 1898–1993 AMERICAN WRITER AND MINISTER

*T*he men I have seen succeed have always been cheerful and hopeful, who went about their business with a smile on their faces, and took all the changes and chances to this mortal life like a man.

Charles Kingsley, 1819–1875 ENGLISH WRITER, POET AND CLERGYMAN

I cannot give you the formula for success,

but I can give you the formula for failure

— which is: try to please everybody.

Herbert Bayard Swope, 1882–1958   AMERICAN NEWSPAPER EDITOR

Success is to be measured not so much by the position one has reached in life, as by the obstacles which one has overcome while trying to succeed.

Booker T. Washington, 1856–1915   AMERICAN TEACHER AND WRITER

Our problem is that we make the mistake of comparing ourselves with other people. You are not inferior or superior to any human being...You do not determine your success by comparing yourself to others, rather you determine your success by comparing your accomplishments to your capabilities. You are 'number one' when you do the best you can with what you have.

Zig Siglar   AMERICAN MOTIVATIONAL WRITER

My formula for success?

Rise early, work late, strike oil.

J. *Paul Getty*, 1892–1976   AMERICAN OIL MAGNATE

You must never conclude, even though everything goes wrong, that you cannot succeed. Even at the worst there is a way out, a hidden secret that can turn failure into success and despair into happiness. No situation is so dark that there is not a ray of light.

Norman Vincent Peale, 1898–1993   AMERICAN WRITER AND MINISTER

What is success?
To laugh often and much;
To win the respect of intelligent people and the affection of children;
To earn the appreciation of honest critics and endure the betrayal of false friends;
To appreciate beauty; To find the best in others;
To leave the world a bit better, whether by a healthy child, a garden patch
or a redeemed social condition;
To know even one life breathed easier because you have lived;
This is to have succeeded.

Ralph Waldo Emerson, 1803–1882   AMERICAN ESSAYIST, POET AND PHILOSOPHER

EXPERIENCE THE JOY OF GIVING

A bit of fragrance always clings to the hand that gives you roses.

Chinese proverb

You find true joy and happiness in life

when you give and give

and go on giving.

Eileen Caddy   CO-FOUNDER OF THE FINDHORN FOUNDATION, SCOTLAND

*I*t is more blessed to give than to receive.

Acts of the Apostles, 20:35

The wise man does not lay up treasure.

The more he gives to others,

the more he has for his own.

Lao-Tze, c. 600 BC   CHINESE PHILOSOPHER AND FOUNDER OF TAOISM

You give but little

when you give of your possessions.

It is when you give of yourself

that you truly give.

Kahlil Gibran, 1883–1931   LEBANESE POET, ARTIST AND MYSTIC

Not what we give, but what we share,

For the gift without the giver is bare.

James Russell Lowell, 1819–1891   AMERICAN POET AND DIPLOMAT

We make a living by what we get,

but we make a life by what we give.

Sir Winston Churchill, 1874–1965   BRITISH STATESMAN AND PRIME MINISTER

The heart of the giver

makes the gift

dear and precious.

Martin Luther, 1483–1546   GERMAN PROTESTANT REFORMER

*T*he only gift is a
portion of thyself.

Ralph Waldo Emerson, 1803–1882   AMERICAN ESSAYIST, POET AND PHILOSOPHER

REFLECT ON YOUR RELATIONSHIPS

Only in relationship can you know yourself,

not in abstraction,

and certainly not in isolation.

Jiddu Krishnamurti, 1895–1986 INDIAN THEOSOPHIST

I am part of all that I have met.

Lord Tennyson, 1809–1892   ENGLISH POET

Once the realisation is accepted that even between the closest human beings infinite distances continue to exist, a wonderful living side-by-side can grow up, if they succeed in loving the distance between them, which makes it possible for each to see the other whole against a wide sky.

Rainer Maria Rilke, 1875–1926   AUSTRIAN POET

*Let there be spaces in
your togetherness.*

Kahlil Gibran, 1883–1931   LEBANESE POET, WRITER, ARTIST AND MYSTIC

I do my thing, and you do your thing,
I am not in this world to live up to your expectations
And you are not in this world to live up to mine.
You are you and I am I,
And if by chance we find each other, it's beautiful.
If not, it can't be helped.

Frederick Salomon Perls, 1893–1970   GERMAN-BORN AMERICAN PSYCHOLOGIST

Well, what is a relationship? It's about two people having tremendous weaknesses and vulnerabilities, like we all do, and one person being able to strengthen the other in their areas of vulnerability. And vice versa. You need each other. You complete each other, passion and romance aside.

Jane Fonda, b. 1937   AMERICAN ACTOR AND POLITICAL ACTIVIST

A man's feeling of good-will towards others is the strongest magnet for drawing good-will towards himself.

Lord Chesterfield, 1694–1773   ENGLISH STATESMAN

You haven't learned life's lesson very well if you haven't noticed that you can give the tone or colour, or decide the reaction you want of people in advance. It's unbelievably simple. If you want them to take an interest in you, take an interest in them first. If you want to make them nervous, become nervous yourself...It's as simple as that. People will treat you as you treat them. It's no secret. Look about you. You can prove it with the next person you meet.

Sir Winston Churchill, 1874–1965   BRITISH STATESMAN AND PRIME MINISTER

The world is a looking-glass,

and gives back to every man

the reflection of his own face.

William Makepeace Thackeray, 1811–1863   BRITISH WRITER

MAGIC OF
THE MIND

The universe is transformation.
Our life is what our thoughts make it.

Marcus Aurelius, 121–180 AD   ROMAN EMPEROR AND PHILOSOPHER

What was once thought

can never be unthought.

Friedrich Durrenmatt, 1921-1990   SWISS WRITER

*E*very revolution

was once a thought

in one man's mind.

Ralph Waldo Emerson, 1803–1882   AMERICAN ESSAYIST, POET AND PHILOSOPHER

A stand can be made against the invasion of an army; no stand can be made against the invasion of an idea.

Victor Hugo, 1802–1885   FRENCH POET AND WRITER

The mind of man is capable of anything — because everything is in it, all the past as well as the future.

Joseph Conrad, 1857–1924   POLISH-BORN ENGLISH WRITER

A man is what he thinks about
all day long.

Ralph Waldo Emerson, 1803–1882   AMERICAN ESSAYIST, POET AND PHILOSOPHER

The mind is an iceberg — it floats with only one-seventh of its bulk above water.

Sigmund Freud, 1856–1939   AUSTRIAN FOUNDER OF PSYCHOANALYSIS

All that we are is the result of what we have thought; it is founded on our thoughts, it is made up of our thoughts. If a man speaks or acts with a pure thought, happiness follows him like a shadow that never leaves him.

Buddha, c. 563–483 BC   INDIAN RELIGIOUS TEACHER AND FOUNDER OF BUDDHISM

Greater than the tread

of mighty armies

is an idea

whose time has come.

Victor Hugo, 1802–1885 FRENCH POET AND WRITER

*W*ith our thoughts

we make the world.

Buddha, c. 563–483 BC   INDIAN RELIGIOUS TEACHER AND FOUNDER OF BUDDHISM

One man

who has a mind and knows it

can always beat ten men

who haven't and don't.

George Bernard Shaw, 1856–1950   IRISH DRAMATIST, ESSAYIST AND CRITIC

FIND TRUTHS
IN BOOKS

Mankind would lose half its wisdom built up over centuries if it lost its great sayings. They contain the best parts of the best books.

Thomas Jefferson, 1743–1826   President of the United States of America

How many a man has dated a new era

in his life from the reading of a book?

Henry David Thoreau, 1817–1862   AMERICAN WRITER

Books are the legacies that a great genius leaves to mankind, which are delivered down from generation to generation as presents to those who are not yet born.

Joseph Addison, 1672–1719   ENGLISH ESSAYIST

Books are the quietest and most constant of friends;

they are the most accessible and wisest of counsellors,

and the most patient of teachers.

Charles W. Eliot, 1834–1926   AMERICAN EDUCATOR

We rely upon the poets, the philosophers and the playwrights
to articulate what most of us can only feel, in joy or sorrow.
They illuminate the thoughts for which we only grope;
they give us the strength and balm we cannot find in ourselves.
Whenever I feel my courage wavering I rush to them.
They give me the wisdom of acceptance,
the will and resilience to push on.

Helen Hayes, 1900–1993   AMERICAN ACTRESS

We read books to find out who we are.
What other people, real or imaginery, do and think
and feel is an essential guide to our understanding
of what we ourselves are and may become.

Ursula LeGuin, b. 1929   AMERICAN SCIENCE FICTION WRITER

All that mankind has done, thought or been

is lying in magic preservation

in the pages of books.

Thomas Carlyle, 1795–1881   SCOTTISH ESSAYIST, HISTORIAN AND PHILOSOPHER

I have never known any trouble that an hour's reading would not dissipate.

Charles Louis de Montesquieu, 1689–1755   FRENCH POLITICAL PHILOSOPHER

When I *am attacked by gloomy thoughts,*

nothing helps me so much as running to my books.

They quickly absorb me and banish the clouds

from my mind.

Michel de Montaigne, 1533–1592   FRENCH ESSAYIST AND PHILOSOPHER

GROW OLD
~ POSITIVELY

Old age is not an illness,

it is a timeless ascent.

As power diminishes,

we grow towards the light.

May Sarton, 1912–1995   AMERICAN WRITER AND POET

Ageing is a life-spanning process of growth and development from birth to death. Old age is an integral part of the whole, bringing fulfilment and self-actualisation. I regard ageing as a triumph, a result of strength and survivorship.

Margaret Kuhn, 1905-1995   AMERICAN CIVIL RIGHTS ACTIVIST

One of the many things nobody ever tells you about middle age is that it's such a nice change from being young.

Dorothy Canfield Fisher, 1879–1958 AMERICAN NOVELIST

Perhaps middle age is, or should be,

a period of shedding shells:

the shell of ambition, the shell of material

accumulations and possessions, the shell of ego.

Anne Morrow Lindbergh, 1906-2001   AMERICAN WRITER

Old age is like a plane flying through a storm.

Once you're aboard, there's nothing you can do.

You can't stop the plane, you can't stop the storm,

you can't stop time. So one might as well

accept it calmly, wisely.

Golda Meir, 1898–1974   ISRAELI PRIME MINISTER

One should never count the years —

one should count one's interests. I have kept young

trying never to lose my childhood sense of wonderment.

I am glad I still have a vivid curiosity

about the world I live in.

Helen Keller, 1880–1968   BLIND AND DEAF AMERICAN WRITER AND SCHOLAR

Published by
The Five Mile Press Pty Ltd
950 Stud Road, Rowville
Victoria 3178 Australia
Email: publishing@fivemile.com.au
Website: www.fivemile.com.au

First published 2000
Reprinted 2001, 2002, 2003, 2004, 2005, 2006, 2007

Editor: Maggie Pinkney
Designer: Zoë Murphy

ISBN 978 1 86503 225 2

Printed in China